That's Deductible!

Simple Tips and Tricks to Find More Business Tax Deductions

Wendy Barlin CPA

Disclaimer

This material & presentation content is for informational and educational purposes only. This material and presentation content is designed to provide general information regarding the subject matter covered. It is not intended to serve as legal, tax, or other financial advice related to individual situations. Because each individual's legal, tax, and financial situation is different, specific advice should be tailored to the particular circumstances.

For this reason, you are advised to consult with your own attorney, accountant, tax preparer, and/or other advisor regarding your specific situation or your client's specific situation. The information and all accompanying material are for your use and convenience only.

PREFACE

Congratulations! You have taken the first step in putting more money in your pocket and understanding how to maximize your business income tax deductions.

I have written this book with you in mind and based on my 25 years' experience in supporting businesses where the two daily questions I heard were always, "How do I know what I can deduct?" and "Have I taken all the deductions that I can?" This book will answer those questions for you.

I have come to offer this advice in a strange and unusual way. I grew up in South Africa and never dreamed of being an author or tax professional. I wanted to be a princess! Sadly, I realized my prince wasn't coming. So I took matters into my own hands and chose a college degree in accounting.

Bored with being a number cruncher after five years, I embarked on an around the world adventure where I met interesting people and saw amazing things. I landed in Los Angeles, California and just fell in love; in love with the energy of the city and the beauty of the California Coastline. So I unpacked my one and only bag, and made California my home.

I learned by trial and error, how to navigate US financial and tax system BUT here I am, 25 years later, having bought and sold several businesses and homes and about to show you how to maximize these benefits for yourself.

With gratitude to my Village, who supported my ideas and brought me to this place of following my dreams.

Here's What's Inside...

Introduction..1

Chapter 1
The Importance of Recordkeeping....................4

Chapter 2
To Deduct or Not to Deduct..............................13

Chapter 3
Deducting your Home Office............................24

Chapter 4
Understanding Estimated Tax Payments.....35

Chapter 5
Are you Missing out on Available Business
Tax Credits?..44

Chapter 6
Exposing the Myths of Incorporating.............53

Chapter 7
The Strategy of Income Tax Planning............67

Our Unique Process..87

How Simple Tips and Tricks
Can Help You Find More Tax
Deductions for Your Business..........................89

Introduction

As a business owner who works hard every day, you show up, you take care of your customers and employees. Just when you think you've covered all bases; you're told at the end of the year you must pay a huge chunk of money in taxes to the government. It wipes out your savings! Not only is this a horrible surprise, depending on the amount you owe, but it can also be a real setback for your business and your life. Surprises like these are emotionally devastating and scary. Where do you turn for help?

If you're like most Americans, you probably still have the old-fashioned CPA you inherited from your parents. Maybe you met him or her at the gym or your local café. He or she seems like a nice person, but busy.

When you finally get a call back, you ask your questions, and you get half-hearted answers. You may not even understand the answers, or even worse, the answers are so confusing you regret calling in the first place. Then you get the bill!

Where do you turn?

So where do you go to learn about maximizing your business deductions? You could ask your neighbor. You could ask another business owner. I guess you could even ask Google. Maybe look at Wikipedia. The problem is your friends are most likely misinformed or working with facts that are no longer true. You can't trust the internet completely either. Worst yet, you hear a joke at the dinner table; someone says, "If you don't pay your taxes, you'll go to jail," or the one I hear all the time, "If you incorporate, you're never going to have to pay taxes." But this one bothers me the most, "Don't take deductions; you'll get audited."

If you're like most small business owners in America, you are busy enough running your business, you do not have time to sift through the facts and myths when it comes to paying taxes. Isn't that what you pay an accountant for? Unfortunately, you may be paying more in taxes than you have to. It's vitally important that you have the proper information when it comes to taxes. My passion is to help you make tax decisions based on facts, not fear.

My hope for you is that you finish this book with a completely new outlook on taxes and managing your money. I want you, as a small business owner, to feel empowered in your choices and to understand how US taxes can affect your business. In this book, I will cover the most commonly asked questions along with the basics of what's deductible and how to take the deductions along with strategies to save you money. It's my desire to show you the options available to you and let you choose how aggressive or conservative you'd like to be within the boundaries of the law.

It's your money and your choice.

Chapter 1
The Importance of Recordkeeping

I can hear you groan when you see the word recordkeeping, but don't skip this chapter. It's vital on so many levels. On a very basic level, I consider it like building your house with bricks or straw. If you build your house with straw and the wind comes up, guess what? Your house is going to fall. If you build your house with bricks, you can withstand any trick the weather may play on you. I liken the straw and brick house to bookkeeping and recordkeeping. If you keep your records like bricks, you are solid and safe. If you keep your records like straw, you leave yourself open to the elements.

Keep Your Receipts

The very first place we start is with receipts themselves. We're going to talk later about actual deductions, but for now, know that securing a deduction is done with a receipt. It no longer has to be a piece of paper. It can be a PDF. The good old days of a big old shoebox of documents or an A through Z filing system is not necessary. You can take a photograph with your phone or scan your receipts. The important thing is that you have a receipt. No receipt, no tax deduction!

Please be aware that a credit card statement or a bank statement is not a receipt.

A receipt is a document, paper or email, from a store or a vendor that itemizes exactly what it is that you purchased. A credit card or bank statement is NOT a receipt. It makes sense, just think about it if you go to any big box store such as Staples, Office Depot or Best Buy, you could buy toilet paper and candy or something personal however the credit card statement just shows the store name, not what you bought and so no way to prove the deductibility of the item. You must keep a receipt so that, if audited, you can show exactly what you bought in that store and how it relates to your business.

However, there is one exception: (tax law loves a good exception!) You do not need a receipt for anything under $25. If you swipe your credit card for a dollar's worth of parking or you buy lunch for $5, for those items, you do not need a receipt. $25 is the cutoff. This is so important because, again, it backs up your deduction.

I suggest keeping receipts in PDF format on a stick drive or in the cloud where you can always access them. Should there be a flood, fire, or other disaster, you are at risk by having a box of paper receipts. In an emergency, having to lug boxes of receipts out of your house or office is no fun. For your sanity, I highly recommend you go with an electronic version of each receipt. Keep all receipts for seven years.

Electronic Records

The next level up of recordkeeping is electronic records for income and expenses. If you are incorporated, you are required by law to keep books and records, double-entry accounting. It's very serious stuff.

When you hear colleagues or friends talking about BOOKKEEPING, they are usually talking about system to record income and expenses for your business. The majority of these systems today are electronic. Our preference is QuickBooks Online but there are literally hundreds of choices of systems available.

I also recommend hiring a professional bookkeeper to manage these systems for you. Can you do it? Sure! Should you do it? NO!!!!!!

Your time and money is better spent hiring a professional. Would you do your own surgery? Remove your own tooth? Install your own plumbing? Then please do not even think about doing your own bookkeeping.

Every error will cost you money.

Still not convinced? I have a client in the real estate business. He came to me with a big, beautiful Excel spreadsheet for the year, and said, "Here's our Excel spreadsheet. We're not incorporated. Can you do our tax return?"

I looked at it, and down at the bottom, it showed a taxable income of $40,000. I said to the client, "How about this? I take this data and put it through our QuickBooks bookkeeping system. If I come up with the same number as you, you don't have to pay me. If my number is different, you pay for our services. Fair?

I entered their data into QuickBooks, and sure enough, they had zero taxable income. Why would their Excel spreadsheet show $40,000 in taxable income, and yet, when we took the same data and put it into a QuickBooks system, it showed no taxable income? Well, here's the issue that we see time and time again. There were two formatting errors in their Excel worksheet. A very large expense was coded as a word and not a number, which causes an error in an addition formula. Wow! Is it worth the risk? How much can you avoid paying a bookkeeper to get clean accurate records and avoid overpaying taxes?

Similarly, I have a client who taught herself to use QuickBooks. Good for her. She spent hours entering her data (when she could have been prospecting for new well-paying clients). OK, no judgement BUT then we sit down to do year-end tax planning and the numbers make no sense. I am asking her questions about her losses and she is stupefied. She didn't believe she had losses.

It was a big pile of dodo. She then spent thousands of dollars to get the work fixed up by a professional bookkeeper AND we missed the tax planning window for her year-end. That was a very expensive lesson.

When I refer to a Professional Bookkeeper, I'm not talking about a friend or neighbor who is a self-taught QuickBooks expert or a tech guru. I am talking about professional bookkeeping from a bookkeeping service where this is what they do all day every day; a person or group of people who are trained in accounting. I promise you this will save you money!

As a tax preparer, when I get reports at the end of the year on which to build the tax return, I don't have the time to go back and audit every line of your bookkeeping. I am pretty sure no CPA would detail review a financial statement before preparing a tax return. None I know of anyway. So what you give a tax preparer to work with is what they use. Scary results if the numbers are not accurate and tax ready.

The tax return is the end of the road for a financial statement. The work is all done before the numbers arrive on the CPA's desk. Remember that please. Promise me that if you learn nothing else from this book, you will hire a professional bookkeeper to manage your accounting system. Please.

I implore you; spending money on bookkeeping is an investment. It is not an overhead.
It is an investment and necessary for your business.

How Much Is It Really Worth?

Here's my other reason for accurate bookkeeping and paying for professional bookkeeping services. When it comes to selling your business, even if you might think, "That's not going to be me," you never know. I have a client who is a doctor based in Los Angeles who was approached by a large Texas medical group to buy his business. They looked at his financial statements, and the doctor called me and said something like this: "Well, you have to add these numbers and not those. Wait, that number is not quite right. Add this line and that line and then subtract that line, and that's what it is."

Well, after going back and forth on this for about three weeks, the buyers walked away and a big opportunity was lost! They said: "These financial statements are not reliable. We cannot make an offer on a business with financials needing to be added and subtracted and moved around." This doctor could have sold his business for millions, but they walked away because his bookkeeping was a mess. The lack of professional bookkeeping can cost you more than tax deductions. It can cost you the sale of your business.

Nobody Wants an Audit

IRS audits are rare, but when they occur, I do my best to prepare for them. In the unlucky event that you are selected for audit, and you have clean books and records, the auditors are way less likely to keep digging if they ask for a report and you can email it in a moment. They've gotten smart, too. They ask for access to QuickBooks or Xero (both online accounting software systems) these days. If they log-in and find clean records, you're much more likely to avoid having them dig deeper and deeper. If you send them a mess, you open up a can of worms. These are the areas where bookkeeping and paying for professional bookkeeping, will save you money in addition to just finding more tax deductions.

If you want to buy or sell a business, you need reliable financials. If you are audited, you need clean financials. If you try to get financing from a bank or any lender, you're going to be asked for financials. The same is true for obtaining loans as for selling your business. Clean, professional financials pays off in loan attainment and preferential interest rates. Go ahead and add up those costs; compare them to the cost of professional bookkeeping. I promise you that professional bookkeeping pays for itself time and time again.

OK OK, I know, move on. But promise, please!

Chapter 2
To Deduct or Not to Deduct

The questions that burn most deeply on every business owner's minds are:

- "Can I deduct that?
- "Have I taken all the deductions I can?"

What I'll tell you is that tax law is broad, very broad. What the law says is that any expense is deductible if it is "ordinary and necessary" for your business.

So now your question should be:

"Is this expense ORDINARY and NECESSARY for my business?"

And if the answer is yes, or you can make a valiant claim of how and why it is, then you have yourself a legitimate business income tax deduction.

However, there are some expenses that are specifically denied. Always exceptions in tax law to keep us on our toes!

I think it's very important to know what those exceptions are and to respect them. There is a great difference between being aggressive for income taxes, pushing ordinary and necessary as far as we can, and doing illegal behavior. We don't ever do illegal behavior. I don't look good in horizontal stripes or the color orange and am certain I would hate the food. I am going to stick within ordinary and necessary.

That's NOT Deductible

A non-deductible expense which always surprises business owners is clothing. <u>Clothing is not deductible.</u> Just because you want to look nice for your job or because you think your clients want you to look a certain way, your clothing purchases are not deductible. Even if you are an actress attending the Academy Awards, the fabulous dress you bought for this special red carpet event, is not deductible.

Clothing is only deductible if it is:

- A uniform.
- It's specifically required for your job by your employer and you would not wear those items in your regular life.
- It has your business's logo or name on it.

Your <u>gym membership is not deductible</u>, ever, end of story. Even if you are a model or an athlete, gym memberships are not deductible. Your <u>golf club dues are also not deductible</u>, not even if you entertain clients at your club. The meals at the club are deductible!

It is very important to understand what is not deductible and not go there. In my experience, if you are found, under audit, to be taking deductions that are against the tax law, you will get the book thrown at you. It will be very hard for us to negotiate any other terms. Let's stick with ordinary and necessary, because I think we can all agree that ordinary and necessary is extremely broad.

Let's be certain that any tax deduction you take is within the law. It is your responsibility as a business owner to take as many deductions as you are allowed. Don't think that by not taking a deduction, you are doing any good for yourself or the world. The way I see it, the more deductions you can take and the more money you can keep in your pocket, the more you can serve yourself and the world.

How Far Can You Go?

I never recommend spending money to get a tax deduction. A call I often get from clients is:

"If I buy a truck is that deductible?"

And my answer is: "Do you need a new truck?"

I prefer to look for income tax deductions within the dollars you are already spending. As you go about your day, and spend money, think to yourself, "Could these expenses be construed as ordinary and necessary for my business?"

For every client that comes into my office, they have a different risk tolerance. Some clients want to never ever risk an audit and they understand that their conservative choices mean they pay more in taxes. Those who choose a more aggressive approach can save significant money in taxes and my job is to assist in minimizing the risk of audit by understanding the fine print of the law.

Imagine for a moment that you happened to stop at three or four different stores and run some errands. What expenses did you incur today which could be construed as ordinary or necessary?

Download the list of deductible expense categories from our website at www.aboutprofit.com

I'm pushing this so hard because, as we talked about in our earlier chapter, every dollar you deduct saves you tax money, puts money back in your pocket that you have worked so hard to earn.

Let me give you an example of how far ordinary and necessary can stretch. I have a client who has a gorgeous little fluffy white dog. It's called a Bichon, and she wanted to deduct all the expenses for keeping her dog in such beautiful shape. This dog needs to be groomed every week. It needs all these very expensive medicines. She put pictures of her dog on her website and her business cards, and he was her business mascot. Crazy? Maybe, but smart!

She did get audited. However, she was able to show that all her pet expenses were ordinary and necessary for her business because her dog is her mascot. He is required to look gorgeous. Does that give you a picture of how far you can stretch ordinary and necessary?

What other examples can you think of in your life? That expensive dinner with your friends who also happen to be business owners? Travel expenses that included meeting with other business owners in your field? Aren't taxes FUN? I love discussing the concept of ORDINARY and NECESSARY!

For you, I recommend taking the time to sit down, look at your current expenses and discuss with your CPA: "What is ordinary and necessary for my business?"

No two businesses are the same. No two business owners are the same. Can you see how just sending your CPA or tax preparer your numbers can effectively be leaving huge amounts of deductions untouched?

Under audit, with your receipts, your records, and a straight face, can you explain why those expenses are ordinary and necessary for your business?

It's Your Business

Let's look at some other interesting examples. Meals? They are always a very grey area. Meals are deductible when they have a business purpose. How is the IRS going to prove your meal did or did not have a business purpose?

How about office supplies? How do they know what was or wasn't used in your office? Candy? Toilet Paper? The list is endless.

Ordinary and Necessary

A good accountant wants to know who you are, how much risk you are willing to take, and how far you want to push that gray area. I have some clients who come into my office who say, "I don't care. I'll pay the taxes. Keep me safe; I never want to get audited." I respect that. We will keep your deductions low, but I will still push you as much as I can to take as many deductions as you are able.

I have other clients who come in and say, "I don't want to pay taxes. I need to grow this business. I want to do things with my money. I'm not paying taxes." Then, my role is to show you how you can do better, show you places where you can push the gray area. It is not my job to tell you what to deduct. It is not my job to put numbers on the tax return that you don't know about. Our job, as accountants and consultants, is to show you your choices and what the risks of those choices are. Then you decide how far you want to go, but we always come back to ordinary and necessary.

Risky Business

I think one of the most important conversations I have with people is about the risk of audit. It seems there is this huge fear of the government and being audited. Audit rates compared to the number of people who file tax returns in the United States are extremely low, especially on the small business owner side and, especially on the incorporated side.

I never recommend making choices for fear of being audited. What I do recommend is file smart tax returns. We put our heads together. We look at what is ordinary and necessary for your business.

Always be sure that you understand your responsibilities and what you are signing. I have had new clients come in and tell me they "just signed" and they have no idea where their prior accountant got those numbers from.

Scary! And can you imagine how the IRS would laugh? NO! Ask questions. Understand every number and why it is on your tax return before you sign.

Let's discuss another word as relates to ORDINARY and NECESSARY: REASONABILITY

As an example, let's assume you bring in $200,000 a year in revenue. If you have $50,000 in meals, does that seem necessary or ordinary for your business? Reasonable? If it is, I recommend you take the deductions to which you are entitled. However, what I am trying to do in analyzing all your expense items is to make sure they all appear ordinary and necessary AND reasonable. Again a reminder that in order to do this, I need accurate numbers!

The IRS no longer has people to run around willy nilly. If you have ever tried to call, nobody answers the phone. Right? The IRS now has very smart computers that are running through tax returns, looking for numbers that are outliers. We want to make sure our numbers are not outliers. If they are, we want to make sure we can explain them. Reasonability!

No one should pass on taking a deduction for fear of an audit. You are leaving money on the table if you knowingly are not taking deductions you could lawfully take. If you have your receipts, and you have good bookkeeping; you can, with a straight face, show that this expense is ordinary and necessary, you take every deduction available to you. And you should!

Chapter 3
Deducting your
Home Office

Probably the most common comment I hear from new clients coming to our office is,
"My prior accountant said if I take a home office, I'm going to get audited".

That makes me cringe. Firstly, that is just not true. It hasn't been true in 25 years. When I first came to this country in 1997, the IRS did show up at your doorstep with a badge, wanting to see your office. They did, and they measured it, and they took pictures and, "Oh, there's a television. That's a no-no." Today, there are over four million home office filers in this country. So, you can relax, nobody is coming over to measure your home office.

Many employees in corporate America are paid and incentivized to work from home. This is no longer a deduction that will trigger an audit. If your accountant is telling you that, he needs to get with the times, and you need to run for the hills to a more modern and educated professional.

A home office deduction is absolutely a valid, reliable deduction you should and must take if you are eligible. As I said in prior chapters, I am not ever going to recommend anything illegal, so it is critical to determine whether you are eligible for this deduction.

There are four million home office filers today. Believe me; the IRS is not going to audit all of them.

What is a Home Office?

A home office is an area of your home where you work. It doesn't have to be a dedicated room, just an area of your home that you work in as your primary office. This is the crux of it, your primary office. Before we talk about the dollars involved, let's talk about whether you are eligible.

There was a court case a few months ago about a doctor who saw patients in his office all day. His office was out in the world on a major street. Then at night and on the weekends he did his billing and some filing at home. He claimed a deduction for home office. He got audited, and IRS said, "No way, this is not your primary office. You have an office, but you choose to come home and work at night, that's your choice."

Let's be very clear about what is your primary office.

I worked with a therapist who had offices on a major boulevard, but her office was set up only to meet with patients. There are no computers there. There's no desk in the space. It's meeting rooms only. Now, she can take a home office because her office is at her home. She does not have any office space where she sees her patients. This is a very important distinction. I also see it in warehousing. If you are a manufacturer and you have a warehouse, do you have an office at the warehouse or is your office at home? Again, primary office.

Office Sharing

Co-working spaces are very popular today, especially with a lot of my social media blogger clients. This has become very interesting. Is that your primary office? This is something I have not yet seen a lot of audits on, but it is something I want to make you aware of. If the IRS were to check your agreement with your co-working space, what does it say? Does it say you've had a designated full-time office? If you do, then I think you're going to struggle to take a home office as well. If it says you have a sharing space, or you can use the collaborative space, then you can with a much clearer conscience, take your home office deduction.

Again, if this is your <u>primary office space</u>, then make sure you discuss this deduction with your CPA. This is not a no-brainer. It's not an easy yes or an easy no. This is one of the critical deductions which can greatly affect your taxable income. It must be determined on a case-by-case basis.

How Much is This Going to Save Me?

Now, let's talk about what dollars are at stake. Let's assume that you are eligible to take a home office deduction. How does it work? There are direct home office expenses and Indirect Home office expenses.

Direct expenses such as painting or repair, that benefit only the area exclusively used in your home for business, are fully deductible.

Indirect expenses are for keeping up and running the entire home, such as insurance, utilities, and general repairs, are indirect expenses that are deductible based on the percentage of the home used for business. Also include your mortgage interest, property taxes and any HOA dues.

Expenses for the part of the home not used for business, such as lawn care or painting a room not used for business, are unrelated expenses that are not deductible.

Telephone expenses for the first home telephone line (if anyone even has those anymore) are nondeductible even if it is used for business. Any additional charges for long distance or a second line into the home used for business are deductible. Any deductible telephone costs are not included as business use of home cost.

Well, now that we have cleared that up, how do you actually calculate your home office deduction? The business percentage equals the area of the part of the home used for business divided by the area of the whole house. Any reasonable method may be used to determine the business percentage.

The following are two common methods.

- Divide square footage of area used for business by total square footage of home.
- If all rooms are about the same size, divide the number of rooms used for business by total number of rooms

That gets a little tricky and grey, because many of us work from home and use not only "an area specifically" but also the dining room table or the kitchen and bathrooms. How do we factor that in?

I refer back to ORDINARY and NECESSARY.

Claiming you use 50% of your home is perhaps precarious unless you can truly make a case for that. The majority of my clients will claim 30% of their home for business use.

Next step is to take your business home percentage and multiply it by the indirect expenses as described above. If we were to take the cost of your home and the mortgage interest or your rent, your utilities, your insurance and say 30% of that applies to your office; does that appear ordinary and necessary?

If you have a business that brings in a couple hundred thousand dollars and your rent for home office is $10,000 a year, which seems reasonable, ordinary, and necessary to me. If your rent turns out to be $50,000, I'm not sure I would use that entire amount because it seems unreasonable as a total or as a percentage of your revenue.

I do have some clients who argue, "I want to take 50% of my home. I work everywhere. I have clients coming to my living room." Again, you can certainly do that if you feel passionate about it and if, under audit, you are comfortable to sit across the table from an IRS agent and explain why you believe that it is ordinary and necessary for you to deduct 50% of your housing expenses against your income. If you can make a case for 50%, more power to you, but most of my clients, instead of measuring the square footage, will take a percentage. Those who choose to be more conservative might go with 10%, 15%, or 20%. Those who want to be more aggressive will take 30% or 35%.

This is definitely a discussion you want to have with your accountant, and you want to look in the mirror and say, "Am I aggressive? Do I want to go to that gray area? I want to take fewer deductions and play it safe."

There is no right or wrong. There's a gray area. How comfortable are you in the gray area?

Finally, let's look at the depreciation of your home office. When you use your home office, you get to depreciate it. That means you get to say, "Well, wow! Now that I'm working from home every day, I'm putting additional wear and tear on my home. I'm going to take the cost of my home and write off a little bit of it every year." It's called depreciation. The math is the county building value of your home, divided by 39 years.

The problem with this deduction is should you ever sell your house down the road, that depreciation gets added back to your cost basis and is not deductible.

I don't always recommend people depreciate their home office, but again, this is something you want to discuss with your tax preparer.

Please don't walk away from the home office deduction because your traditional accountant was uninformed or misinformed about your eligibility. Have the discussion and make sure, if this is your primary office that you go ahead and take the deduction that applies to you.

I have a client who built an extra dwelling unit on their property. She turned her garage into a home office. This is a real home office. It is separated from the actual physical home. However, this same client bought $8,000 worth of artwork to hang on the wall to make their office look gorgeous. She also bought a refrigerator so she wouldn't have to go into the main house to get drinks and snacks throughout the day. These are deductible, but do they appear ordinary and necessary? This client wanted to be very aggressive and said, "Yes. I need to deduct these, and if I get audited, I will explain to the auditor why these are ordinary and necessary expenses for my primary office." I probably wouldn't have gone that far, but again, everybody has a line in the sand. I had another client who deducted the blinds they put up in their home office room. They were expensive, but it was getting too hot in there to work, so that was necessary. What do you think is reasonable and necessary for your office space?

And lastly, please be aware that the home office deduction is limited to your business income. This means that you cannot use your home office deduction to create a business loss. The unused expenses can however be carried forward.

Running Errands

Did you know when you drive from home to work every day, that's called commuting, and that's not deductible mileage? Fact!

When you drive from your office to see clients, go to a class, or to a meeting, the mileage deductible. That's business mileage, and it is deductible under the law.

So, when you have a home office, any time you leave your home you are effectively leaving your office right? Nice!

Taking a home office deduction now also opens a huge category of automobile and travel expenses.

Let's assume you go to pick up your children from school, but you stopped at the post office to mail a package to a client. That entire roundtrip, under the law, is a business mileage deduction.

What are the other examples in your daily life you can think of where you leave your Home Office to run errands?

To be fair, you can't claim that 100% of your car is deductible and 100% of your gas and your mileage are deductible. You have a personal life, or we would hope you do.

The auto deduction is either, cents per business mile and the IRS changes that rate each year. Or, you can choose to take a business percentage of gas/insurance/maintenance being actual expenses incurred. On audit, you would need to prove your business mileage. I recommend keeping your calendar for the last seven years which will show every appointment and meeting you drove to and then a note of other errands traveled on each day. There are also some fabulous inexpensive apps that you can download onto your cell phone that track your mileage so that you always have records of your business mileage.

The percentage of business mileage; exactly how much to deduct is another discussion to have with your accountant and consider your risk tolerance. How much of your driving truly is business versus personal? How aggressive are you willing to be to keep more money in your pocket?

Remember, the principle is that, when you take a home office, every time you drive from your office outbound, you're creating a deduction, while when you drive to an office that is commuting. This is not money we're spending to create deductions. This is money we're spending in any event; we're just converting it to be deductible.

Chapter 4
Understanding Estimated Tax Payments

Federal income tax is a pay-as-you-go tax. You must pay the tax as you earn or receive income during the year. There are two ways to pay as you go, either by employer withholding or estimated tax payments.

As an employee, you had income taxes withheld from your paycheck and now as an employee of your corporation you also have income taxes withheld from your paycheck.

Estimated tax is the method used to pay tax on income that is not subject to withholding, for example, the taxable profit of your business. If you don't pay enough by the due date of each quarterly payment period you may be charged a penalty even if you are due a refund when you file your tax return. It sounds crazy I know and most clients look at me like I am from Mars when I explain this rule. I don't make the rules, I just help explain and enforce them!

Estimated taxes are calculated as 90% of the tax to be shown on your current year tax return, or 100% of the tax shown on your previous year's tax return. I always recommend the most conservative approach is to pay 100% of the previous year's federal income tax in quarterly estimates if you are someone who hates paying penalties. Many of my clients, including me, choose to take a more aggressive stance and we don't pay estimated taxes. We choose to hold onto our cash all year long to weather the storm of business (the ups and downs of cash flow) and then we pay in what we actually owe before the deadline. YES, we pay penalties. To me, the security of having the cash in my bank account all year long if I need it far outweighs the penalties incurred. But that's just me, and about 80% of my clients. I don't judge. We discuss and we decide what the most prudent approach is for you.

About twenty years ago when I worked in traditional large CPA firms, we were taught to have clients overpay their estimates and then get large refunds when we filed their actual tax returns. We looked like heroes! Sadly, we were not heroes at all; we were simply overpaying taxes and using the government as a savings tool for our clients. Today I stay far away from those tactics and prefer to never have the IRS hold our money in large amounts or for longer than is necessary!

The importance of this chapter is to understand. Understand how much you are required to pay in estimated taxes and then understand the penalties associated if you choose not to make those payments. I raise this point as I have had many irate clients yelling at me over the years as they did not understand this properly and were devastated at even having to pay $1 in penalties. Make sure you ask, ask and ask again until you are clear on how the estimated income taxes work.

Payment Due Dates

For estimated tax purposes, the year is divided into four payment periods. Each period has a specific payment due date.

- First installment : January 1 to March 31, Payment Due April 15th
- Second installment : April 1 to May 31, Payment Due June 15th
- Third installment : June 1 to August 31, Payment Due September 15th
- Fourth installment: September 1 to December 31, Payment due January 15th (of the following year!)

I recommend you always make these payments online at **www.irs.gov**. You will receive an email confirmation of payment.

You Won't' Go to Jail

Now, let's talk about the world of the business owner because sometimes our world can be very different. As I said earlier, many of my clients, including me, don't make estimated payments. I know you're going to find that shocking and horrifying. I promise you, none of us is going to jail. There's no jail for not paying estimated tax payments. There may be a penalty. The penalty is calculated on Form 2210 for Individuals and Form 2220 for corporations. That is where you must decide your plan of action.

Here's the anomaly as a business owner. Last year, you might have had a phenomenal year and had to pay a lot in taxes, which means your estimated taxes for this year are high based on last year. If the current year is slower, your profits are less, you're investing in some new equipment, or the tax law has changed, and you are paying last year's estimates, then you are overpaying in the current year and must wait to file the taxes to get your refund. That doesn't seem like smart cash flow planning to me. Remember cash, green money, eclipses tax decisions every time!

Many of my clients choose to meet with me every three months and look at how much money they've made. We run a tax projector and say, "What is it you would likely owe today based on your current numbers?" That's what we send to the government. Actual amounts due.

Those who want to be even more aggressive won't send that amount to the government. They'll essentially put it in a savings account. Then, we meet the next quarter again and do the same thing, run a projection. "What are you likely to owe? Do we have enough money set aside and then decide? Do we send it in, or do we leave it in a savings account?" We continue this until we get to a point in the year where we're very confident and certain that this is what we're going to owe.

To do this level of hands on tax planning requires two things:

1. Up to date and accurate financial records (Review Chapter on Recordkeeping!)
2. An accountant who enjoys the planning and strategy and will meet with you quarterly to do this work. Will have to pay for the service but it will put money in your pocket!

We send it to the government when we know what we owe; that way, we never overpay.

Why All the Penalties

The reason you will get penalized is the government wants their money every three months. Much like any other business, they need cash flow. The government cannot wait until April every year to get your money. They need the cash flow every month. Even if you pay 100% by April 15th, you will still be penalized because they wanted the money every three months.

The other important thing to know is that an extension is an extension to file and not an extension to pay. Very often, people come to me extremely upset when we figure out what they owe in June or July, and they say, "But I'm on an extension." I have to explain that an extension is an extension of time to file. All taxes are due by April 15th. If you don't pay by April 15th, the penalties are much more substantial than they are for missing estimated payments.

We can play around with estimated payments as a tax and cash flow strategy, but we always pay what's due by April 15th.

One of my favorite strategies for tax and cash flow planning, as it relates to taxes, is the book Profit First by Mike Michalowicz. I am a Profit First Professional, which means I am authorized to teach the Profit First method. It is the only strategy I have come across in 25 years which works. My clients who actively set aside a percentage of their gross revenue every month, are always able to pay their taxes when due. And it's set aside in a bank account that you don't see on your banking app every day. That way the money is "gone" from your world and doesn't get mistakenly used for a vacation or new car.

Don't Spend it All

The biggest issue I come across when clients decide to take the risk by not paying quarterly estimates is that come April, they don't have the cash to pay taxes because they've spent it.

Not only do you need to be okay with paying a penalty, you need to be a good cash manager. You must make a commitment that you will have the cash to pay the taxes. That's why when I meet with clients every quarter, I insist on also making sure that not only do they know what they owe, but they have it in a savings account. This is because come April you must have that cash to pay. The risk of not paying every quarter with my business owners is some fabulous business idea or wonderful opportunity comes along, and they spend the money.

Right now, I'm helping a doctor who's in that very situation. He's a very successful pediatric doctor in Los Angeles. Towards the end of 2018, he found the opportunity to buy the condo of his dreams. He went ahead and used all his available cash as a down payment on this condo. He got an awesome rate and a great deal on the condo. Everything was good in the world until he spoke to me in December, and I asked him, "Where is our tax money?" He said, "Well, I used it to buy my condo. It's gone." Now he had to come up with the money for all of 2018's taxes by April 15th, 2019.

Everything I'd helped him save he'd used to buy the condo. Now, we are playing catch-up. He's paying penalties, big ones. Cash management is integral when you take an aggressive stance as it relates to estimated payments.

The estimated payments can be set up to run automatically on the internet. The government has made it very easy for people to go online and set up their estimated payment for the entire year to run through a bank account. It's safer than sending a check in the mail. I see so much check fraud where checks are being stolen out of the mail, duplicated on high-end copiers and then presented and cashed. Your check may never make it to the IRS.

If you go onto the government website and make a direct payment from your bank account to theirs, there is no fee. The payment is made on time. You have proof of payments. I have not seen any fraud thus far using that system. The site is www.irs.gov.

Chapter 5
Are you Missing out on Available Business Tax Credits?

Do you even know there are credits available for small businesses like yours? Most clients I meet with don't, even if they come to me from very large CPA firms. For whatever reason, business tax credits don't seem to get a lot of press. You don't see anything about them on the news because business credits cost the government money. They are available to you, but nobody is pushing you to take them, and certainly not the government, it costs the government money every time they give you a credit.

Every year, there are business tax credits passed and allowable to all sorts of businesses in all areas. It is our responsibility to know what business you're in, what credits are available, and make you aware of them. If you have not had that discussion with your accountant, you are hurting yourself, and they are doing you a disservice. It is very important every year to discuss with your accountant what business tax credits are available and may be applicable for you and your business. Tax credits change every year, so you need to research what's available and applicable every year.

I had a client referred to me from a very large CPA firm based in Los Angeles, a multimillion-dollar marketing firm. I looked at their tax return. They did not take any credits for which they were eligible. When I raised the issue with them, they'd never heard of the credits, and their prior accountant never offered any to them. I filed for these business tax credits and in just one year, we saved them $50,000 in federal taxes. That ought to get your attention! Fortunately, we are allowed to amend tax returns and that means getting credits for the last three years. Do you think they are happy clients? This is a conversation you absolutely must-have. The General Business Credit Form is 3800 in your Federal corporate income tax return.

Nobody Tells the Business Owner

The other thing the IRS tells accountants about, but not necessarily you, is that they issue reports on their website, www.irs.gov, which detail all the credits that are available. Simply checking a box on your business or personal tax return could get you additional business tax credits.

The IRS lets us know how many millions of dollars are left on the table because these credits are missed. Do you want to be one of those people who lost out? I think not. These are discussions that are imperative to have. These credits are broad. They are for software companies, technology companies, manufacturing, and research, for what part of the city you're in, for vehicles that you buy. Please don't go to Google or Wikipedia for this information. It changes all the time. There is no certainty that the internet stays current and that articles you find are current for today's existing credits. This is something you must discuss with your accountant who should be keeping up with credit tax credits.

It's All in the Numbers

I'm a big proponent of using software instead of a CPA to do your taxes. If you are extremely risk-averse and you don't want to play in the gray area, then I often recommend my clients use some of the out-of-the-box tax preparation software. They're very good. Those companies spend millions of dollars perfecting the software. If you follow the system, you will file an accurate and appropriate tax return. What those systems don't do is understand the business that you're in and whether any tax credits will be appropriate for you.

An example would be a client who is in the software development business but not necessarily building an app. Perhaps they are helping clients effectively build out software. They can get research and development credits. Many of my techies don't even know that these credits are available to them.

Figuring out whether you can get a credit, much like getting a mortgage or a loan, doesn't cost you money out of pocket. If it turns out you are not eligible for the credit, then you don't pay anything at all. It is worth investing the time to figure out what credits are available. There is no downside. If it's a no, it costs you nothing. If it's a yes, you save a lot of money.

On the next page I have included the list of business credits available today. This list may change year to year but it will give you an idea of how many credits are available. It's a long list! There may be one or more for which you are eligible. Make sure you present this list to your accountant.

Business Credits Chart

CREDIT	Form	IRS Pub.	Irc
Alternative Fuel Vehicle Refueling Property Credit Property other than buildings used to dispense clean-burning fuel into vehicles: • Non-hydrogen refueling property. • Hydrogen refueling property.	8911	334	30C
Alternative Motor Vehicle Credit Energy efficient vehicles.	8910	334	30B
Biodiesel and Renewable Diesel Fuels Credit Production, use, sale of qualified fuels.	8864	334	40A
Biofuel Producer Credit Production, use, sale of qualified fuels.	6478	334	40
Carbon Oxide Sequestration Credit Capture and disposal of carbon oxide.	8933	334	45Q
Credit for Employer Differential Wage Payments Wages paid to uniformed service members.	8932	334	45P
Credit for Employer-Provided Childcare Facilities and Services Buy, build, or expand childcare facility.	8882	334	45F
Credit for Employer Social Security and Medicare Taxes Paid on Certain Employee Tips Amount paid on tips exceeding $5.15 per hour.	8846	334	45B

CREDIT	Form	IRS Pub.	Irc
Credit for Increasing Research Activities Research and experimental costs.	6765	334	41
Credit for Small Employer Pension Plan Start-Up Costs Establishment of new pension plan.	8881	560	45E
Disabled Access Credit Creating access for the disabled.	8826	334	44
Distilled Spirits Credit Wholesale distilling, importing, storage of distilled spirits.	8906	334	5011
Employer Credit for Paid Family and Medical Leave Paid FMLA leave to qualified employees.	8994	334	45S
Empowerment Zone Employment Credit Wages paid in certain geographic areas.	8844		1396
Energy Efficient Home Credit Home construction contractor sales.	8908	334	45L
Enhanced Oil Recovery Credit Qualified costs of enhanced oil recovery.	8830		43
Indian Employment Credit Wages and health insurance costs paid to Indian tribe employees.	8845	334	45A
Investment Credit	3468	334	
Rehabilitation Credit Buildings placed in service before 1936 or historic structures.			47

CREDIT	Form	IRS Pub.	Irc
Qualifying Advanced Coal Project Credit IRS approved advanced coal projects.			48A
Qualifying Gasification Project Credit IRS approved projects to convert coal, biomass, or other materials into gas.			48B
Qualifying Advanced Energy Project Credit IRS approved property placed in service for advanced energy projects.			48C
Low-Income Housing Credit Provision of low-income residential property.	8586	334	42
Mine Rescue Team Training Credit Costs for training qualified employees.	8923	334	45N
New Markets Credit Qualified community development.	8874	334	45D
Orphan Drug Credit Research and testing on drugs for rare diseases.	8820	334	45C
Qualified Plug-In Electric Drive Motor Vehicle Credit Qualified plug-in electric drive vehicles. • Four-wheeled plug-in electric vehicles. • Two-wheeled plug-in electric vehicles.	8936		30D
Qualified Railroad Track Maintenance Credit Railroad track maintenance expenditures.	8900	334	45G

CREDIT	Form	IRS Pub.	Irc
Credit for Small Employer Health Insurance Premiums Small employer health insurance premiums.	8941		45R
Work Opportunity Credit Employment of targeted individuals.	5884		51
Credit for Federal Tax Paid on Fuels Off-highway fuel use.	4136	510	34
Credit for Prior Year Minimum Tax—Corporations Minimum tax credit.	8827	542	53

Chapter 6
Exposing the Myths of
Incorporating

I get this question every day, "If I incorporate, will I avoid paying taxes?" I wish that were the case. It's not. Incorporating does save you taxes, but it does not mean you don't pay any taxes at all. You'll still pay taxes. The other important thing about incorporating that all business owners need to understand is that the same ordinary and necessary deductions we talked about a few chapters ago apply whether you are incorporated or not. Everybody has the same deductions available to them. The same laws apply to your home office, ordinary and necessary, and about business deductions, whether you are incorporated or not, I want to be extremely clear about that.

What You Can and Can't Avoid

By incorporating you can avoid some self-employment taxes. Businesses that are not incorporated pay full-boat 15% self-employment taxes. That's Social Security and Medicare from their profit. When you incorporate, you can save a large portion of those self-employment taxes. For every business, it's a different savings. Some businesses can save as much as half of their self-employment taxes, others less. It's important to understand the biggest savings with a corporation is the self-employment taxes. It is not an additional deduction. The deductions are the same.

There are legal issues to consider when you incorporate. I would encourage all business owners to seek legal counsel to learn about the legal responsibilities associated with self-employment and incorporation. A corporation can protect you against vendors or against being sued, and it's very important to understand what those protections are.

In addition, 1099s are not issued for corporations. When you do work for your clients and are not incorporated, clients must send you a 1099 for the work done. You then declare all the money you earned during the year.

The 1099 is the form the IRS uses to track income and make sure everybody is paying what they're supposed to on the income they earned. We declare all the money we make. We pay tax on it. Period.

The problem is that 1099s are so unreliable. They often don't arrive, or they are incorrect. Then you are left communicating with the government back and forth over why the 1099s received don't match your taxable income.

Corporations do not receive 1099s. Corporations declare income based on what they earned. Incorporating saves you money, but keep in mind that you deduct all the same expenses as unincorporated businesses.

One other thing to consider is that audit rates on corporations are much lower than on individuals. Because of the costs and paperwork involved with incorporating, the IRS generally finds people who are incorporated are toeing the line, keeping good records, keeping copies of their deduction receipts, taking available and proper deductions. People who are truly small business owners, but choose not to incorporate, often are doing things a little more loosely, may not keep good records, do proper bookkeeping, nor keep receipts.

The IRS tends to audit more often businesses that make or show a profit of $100,000 or less on an unincorporated return. That doesn't make sense to most of us who say, "Well, if they want to go get more tax money, why wouldn't they go after the big businesses?" It's much more challenging to go after the big businesses. It's much easier to go after the small, unincorporated business and find more money.

I had a client who was a trust fund kid. Her parents paid all her bills so she lived in Beverly Hills. One year, she received an audit notice. The IRS wanted her to prove how she was able to live in the 90210 zip code and yet her tax return only showed taxable income of $25,000. There were no additional taxes to be found for the IRS by the audit but the stress and anxiety was unpleasant for my client.

What is an S Corporation?

By far the most popular form of corporation I see today is the S Corporation. S corporations are corporations that elect to pass income, losses, deductions, and credits through to their shareholders for federal tax purposes. Shareholders of S corporations report the flow-through of income and losses on their personal tax returns and are assessed tax at their individual income tax rates. This allows S corporations to avoid double taxation on the corporate income. Why is this important? Well, if you elect to be a C Corporation which is the older more traditional corporate entity, then the corporation itself pays tax on its profits. When you draw those profits out of the corporation, you pay taxes again!

This makes the flow through entity of the S Corporation very desirable for most business owners as they only pay income taxes one time, on their personal tax return.

Now, there is always a BUT in tax law. A C Corporation does have additional deductions that an S Corporation does not have for example medical reimbursements and health insurance for the shareholders. C Corporations also have lower audit rates. I highly recommend you discuss the best and most appropriate entity for you and your family before allowing public opinion or hearsay to decide for you.

Probably the biggest issue with S Corporations that is not understood by 99% of the business owners who come in to see me is that the IRS required that the owner of an S Corporation must be paid reasonable wages for the duties performed. Even with a single-shareholder corporation, federal and state payroll taxes must be withheld and a year-end W-2 must be submitted, just as with any other employee.

What are "Reasonable Wages?"

Reasonable wages by definition is extremely broad and open to interpretation. Much like ordinary and necessary. Getting the feeling that tax law is grey? Yes, me too!

Under audit, I have seen the IRS ask for comparable salaries for the same work in order to assess reasonability. Again, reasonable is a term worth discussing with your accountant. I know zero is not reasonable and 100% of profit is not reasonable but anything in between is up for discussion, in my opinion.

Are Partnerships an Entity?

Partnerships are not a separate entity like a corporation. A partnership is the relationship existing between two or more persons who join together to carry on a trade or business. Each person contributes money, property, labor, or skill and expects to share in the profits and losses of the business. A partnership must file an annual information return to report the income, deductions, gains, or losses from its operations, but it does not pay income tax. Instead, it passes through any profits or losses to its partners. Each partner includes his or her share of the partnership's income or loss on his or her tax return.

Unlike an S Corporation, partners are not employees and should not be issued a Form W-2 (or a Form 1099). The partnership must furnish copies of Schedule K-1 (Form 1065) to the partners to be used for their own tax filings. The partnership itself does not pay federal income tax. Partners of a partnership (and or LLC), will put payroll taxes (being Medicare and Social Security taxes) on their entire share of partnership income. This can get expensive. Is a partnership the best tax vehicle for your business? Both a legal and tax opinion are required here!

Is an LLC a Corporation?

On a daily basis I get calls from prospective clients who have set themselves up as LLC's after doing online research. Groan! LLC's are easy and inexpensive to set up but are often the most expensive tax vehicle, depending on which state you operate in. Please make sure you get expert advice about your specific situation before spending any money to form an LLC!

An LLC may be classified for federal income tax purposes as a partnership, corporation, or an entity disregarded as separate from its owner. An LLC with at least two members is classified as a partnership for federal income tax purposes.

An LLC with only one member is treated as an entity disregarded as separate from its owner for income tax purposes. This means that the owner includes their LLC on their own personal tax return and the LLC does not file its own Federal income tax return.

If an LLC does not choose to be classified under the above default classifications, it can elect to be classified as an association taxable as a corporation or as an S corporation. After an LLC has determined its federal tax classification, it can later elect to change that classification. See IRS Form 8832, Entity Classification Election.

An individual owner of an LLC treated as a disregarded entity is not an employee of the LLC. The owner is subject to self-employment tax on the net earnings in the same manner as a sole proprietorship. This can get very expensive as you are now adding approximately 15% to your tax bill. Will electing to be taxed as a corporation save you tax money? Perhaps, certainly worth discussing with your CPA.

How do I get Money out of My Business?

As the shareholder of a corporation, you can take a salary from your corporation and pay payroll taxes on that salary (Medicare and social security taxes) and as discussed, you do need to take a reasonable salary.

You as the shareholder can take a dividend from the corporation. Dividends are then taxed on your personal income tax return but at a lower rate than "earned income". That is certainly a consideration worth discussing.

In addition, you as the shareholder can take a loan from the corporation. This loan is not taxable to you but you will need to sign a loan document or have a legal minute allowing loans to and from the corporation at whatever interest rate you choose. Sounds good right? Yes, loan yourself money! As long as the loan doesn't become "unreasonable" and market rate interest is being charged, you are within the law.

"Reasonable Wages"

Earlier in this chapter we referenced the IRS law requiring corporations to issue their shareholders a "reasonable wage". For C corporations and S corporations, there are incentives to skew wages one way or the other for purposes of tax savings. In a C corporation, wages are deductible by the corporation but dividends are not, creating incentive for a C corporation shareholder to inflate the wages for higher deductions.

In an S corporation, wages are subject to payroll taxes but flow-through income is not, creating an incentive for artificially low wages. Both C corporations and S corporations are required by law to pay "reasonable wages," which approximate wages that would be paid for similar levels of services in unrelated companies.

Intermingling Funds

One of the most dangerous financial mistakes a business owner can make is to intermingle funds, such as paying personal expenses from the business checking account, or paying business expenses from the owner's personal account. This can be done with the best of intentions with the business owner making adjustments in the books to separate the business and personal transactions, but the behavior can leave openings for the IRS or courts to question the integrity of the business entity or the transactions. Failure to maintain complete financial separation between a business and its owners is one of the major causes of tax and legal trouble for small businesses.

The Downside of Incorporating

It would behoove us to talk about the downsides of incorporating. I spend a lot of my time discussing with clients what they are taking on. Once we debunk the myth that incorporating is going to mean you pay no taxes and talk about the practicalities of what it means to be incorporated and what's going to happen, many clients will change their mind, and here's why. Being incorporated is a lot more paperwork. You have to put on your adult shoes and step up your business management.

As discussed earlier, this means running yourself a salary. Running a salary probably sounds simple but there is a lot of paperwork required to make that happen.

As a corporation, running your payroll is a deluge of paperwork.

As a corporation you will be filing quarterly payroll documents with the government, figuring out how much tax to pay in, when to file the forms and what is reasonable. Payroll is one of the major issues small businesses run into.

There are other legal requirements and documentation requirements when you incorporate based on your state. Every state has different rules; every city has different rules on how they deal with incorporated entities. Then your accountant is going to have to file a separate tax return. If you incorporate, you're paying for another tax return because the corporation stands alone and files its own tax return. And then of course let's not forget my other favorite topic, recordkeeping! Corporations are required to keep books and records.

Will Incorporating Save You Money?

Yes, but you must be clear about your responsibilities. I have many clients who make a lot of money and have chosen not to incorporate. They're paying a lot of money in Social Security and Medicare tax. Every year, I beg them, "Please, incorporate. I know I can save you half of your self-employment tax." They say to me, "We don't have the time for the paperwork." They don't want to deal with the paperwork. "I like my life. Every couple of weeks, I deposit my money. I put it through QuickBooks. It's no big deal. I don't need the headache. That's okay."

This is where it comes down to your accountant knowing you and you knowing yourself. It's like we talked about in the estimated payments. Will you do whatever it takes to save a dollar? Will you do whatever it takes to save $5,000? Every client that I speak to has a different line in the sand of what a dollar means to them. Lots of clients will go through the incorporation hassle and drama to save a dollar. Others won't touch it even if I can save those 10.

I think it's very important to understand that incorporating doesn't mean you don't pay taxes.

It means your taxes are different. You can save money on taxes, but it's not a slam dunk. It's a lot of paperwork and for the same deduction. You have to look at your day and your life and say, "How much additional work am I willing to do to get the savings?" There's no right or wrong here.

Based on my experience, everybody who has incorporated has saved money. They have seen their business grow because there is something that happens to your revenue and your level of business when you make the decision to step up and incorporate. Focusing on your business and making it a priority, and making it adult and legitimate with incorporation and the federal ID number, seems to help my clients grow as well.

That's not a tangible effect of incorporating, but I see a leveling up in business for those who decide to take that leap. I am always on the side of incorporation. Let me show you another way to run your business, but we must have the discussion of how much extra work this is and what it is going to cost. A rule of thumb: When your taxable income is about $50,000, that's when you're usually ready to discuss how to start saving money truly.

Chapter 7
The Strategy of Income Tax Planning

I have left the most important chapter for last. For those of you who start a book at the back, and I know there are some of you, then you have started at my favorite chapter.

Tax planning is the most valuable work I do with clients. If you are running a business and you only see your accountant once a year to get your income tax return prepared, you are, without doubt, leaving money on the table. I say that categorically and with a guarantee. The majority of small business owners are cash basis taxpayers. What that means is that you pay tax on cash you deposit less monies spent. I would also like you to be aware of a very interesting tax concept that many business owners are unaware of: The Constructive Receipt.

Income is constructively received when an amount is credited to the taxpayer's account or made available to the taxpayer without restriction. The taxpayer does not need to have possession of the income. If someone is authorized to be an agent and receive income for the taxpayer, the taxpayer is considered to have received it when the agent received it. Income is not constructively received if control or its receipt is subject to substantial restrictions or limitations.

So what that means in regular English is that holding a check or postponing taking possession of payment in whatever form, from one tax year to another does not postpone constructive receipt. Business expenses are deducted in the tax year they are actually paid, even if they were incurred in an earlier year.

Example: Ken is an excavator and reports income and expenses under the cash method. On December 26, 2018, he receives a check in the mail for services performed in September 2018. Ken deposits the check into his business checking account on January 5, 2019. The income is includable on his 2018 tax return. Got it?

This makes for an interesting discussion about year-end tax planning. Our goal is to decide which tax year we want income and or expenses to fall into. The decision hinges on many factors such as your goals, do you want to buy a house or get a loan for which you need high income on your tax return. Or, are you just about to bridge to a new tax bracket. Not doing effective tax planning can be disastrous if you find yourself within a new tax bracket that could have been avoided.

Are You a Cash Basis Taxpayer?

Please make sure you know. If a business produces, purchases, or sells merchandise, the business must keep an inventory and generally use the accrual method for sales and purchases. The gross receipts test allows taxpayers with average annual gross receipts that do not exceed $25 million for the three prior tax-year period to use the cash method.

Under the accrual method of accounting, a taxpayer generally reports income in the year earned and deducts or capitalizes expenses in the year incurred. The purpose of the accrual method is to match income and related expenses in the same year. It is critical that you know on which basis your business income tax return is filed.

So you can see how one date in the calendar, being the calendar year-end of December 31st which is also likely your business year-end, is a critical time. By making deposit on the last day of the year, you incur additional taxes. Paying a business expense of the last day of the year, you reduce that year's taxes. This makes for many strategic choices in working with your accountant.

We insist that we meet with every client in the last quarter of the year. Our last quarter of the year is busier than our tax season because the real work is done in the last quarter and the last month.

The First Piece of the Puzzle

Let's assume a tax bracket caps at $200,000. We do no tax planning, the year-end closes, and you go off to see your accountant in February with your beautiful set of financials created by your professional bookkeeper that shows a taxable income of $201,000. That's a very sad day. That means that, because of that $1,000 over the bracket, your entire income is now taxed 3% more than it would have been if you had found one more thousand-dollar deduction in December. We don't want that to happen.

We meet with every single client in the last quarter of the year to look at their financial statements and we ask:

- Where are we?
- How much cash do you have set aside for taxes?
- Where are you within your bracket?
- What are your goals?

Perhaps we should start by talking about the goal because I think this is often one that's forgotten both by clients and accountants because we're so focused on taxes. "What are we going to pay? I don't have the cash. I don't want to spend more money." Your goals are often affected by your tax returns.

Think of all the uses of income tax returns in your life:

- Buy a house.
- Buy a business.
- Refinance a house.
- Refinance a loan.

Even on the immigration front or the health insurance side, you're often called upon to show your tax returns. The list goes on and on.

Now, if you tell your accountant next year, "I am going to buy a house, refinance a house, buy a business," then we can be strategic about the tax return that we filed. Now, to be very clear, we must declare all the income we earned. That's the law. We must declare all the income we earned. We don't do anything illegal ever.

You Don't Have to Take Deductions

We are not required by law to take every deduction we're entitled to. You are most welcome to overpay your taxes. If your strategy is to buy a business next year or get a loan and you need a tax return that shows a certain income number to do that, we can do that by taking certain expenses or deferring expenses to the following year. This is where planning and goals are critical. You absolutely must, first, know what your own goals are, which is another whole book. Then, share those goals with your accountant so that you can plan for them.

Cash Flow Management

The second reason for strategic income tax planning is cash flow management. This is a yearlong process but most important towards the end of the year. If we do nothing, we run a projection that says, "If we do nothing based on the financials I'm looking at, it looks like this is what you'll owe come April. Do you have it?" That answers two questions. One, "Yes, I do. Should I pay it now or in April?" That would be your choice depending on cash flow. Two, "Oh no, I don't have it." Then the discussion is, "Well, can you figure out how to get it before April or do we need to be very cognizant over the last few months of the year about what we deposit and what we spend?" We go into the holiday season knowing exactly what our holiday budget can be and that's the bonus news.

How to Show More or Less Income

So the question I am most often faces with by clients is "If I want to show less income on my tax return, how do I do that?"

How you're going to do that is by not invoicing your clients in December. Invoice them in January. Don't deposit checks in December. Take a vacation, close the office. These are the strategies that are completely legal and can be deployed in the last quarter of the year. You can also prepay a whole lot of expenses in December. If we find that your taxable income is too high for the year, and we're bouncing a bracket, often what we'll do is look at bills you ordinarily would have paid the first week in January and pay them in December.

Now remember, all you are really doing is affecting your income tax return for that year. By taking this strategy, you are creating income in January and risk inflating the next year's tax problem. So please do be careful and make sure you analyze all the ins and outs of these strategies as they relate to you, your business and your cash situation.

If you want to show more income on your tax return, then what will you do in December? You will invoice all your clients and customers, and you will get that money in your bank account by December 31st.

Capital Purchases

December is a great month for holiday sales. Everywhere we look, it's a sale. It's a deal. Buy two, get one free. Very often, we are excited and grabbed by the American marketing machine to spend money in December. If your business needs new computers or needs a new truck, those can be substantial expenses. Does it make sense to buy them in December or buy them in January? These are the discussions you absolutely must have with your accountant.

It is so disappointing to me when clients don't ask and just buy a new truck for their business in the last week of December and ruin not only the current year's tax plan but also the following year where they may have better used the deduction. Please don't get wrapped up in the marketing machine and stick to your tax strategy.

Having lived here for 25 years and been subject to the same marketing and advertising that you have. I have come to learn that there is always another deal around the next corner!

In the grand scheme of things, it doesn't matter whether you get the truck in December or January because it's only a few weeks that you will not have it. That December 31st deadline is critical for when you buy those purchases.

Again, I wanted to have the most common discussions about our trucks, computers, larger purchases (called Capital Purchases for income taxes) that could fall on either side of December 31st. Do you wait for the January sales or do you take advantage of the December sale? Do you need the deduction in this year, or do you need the deduction next year? These are really, important discussions to have, and they affect not only cash flow, but they affect taxes, and they affect the running of your business.

Keep More Cash in your Pocket.

My goal is to minimize your taxes by maximizing your income tax deductions. This means, we also have to talk about cash flow and business goals. What are we trying to do here? Strategies are critical to every business owner and the deductions they do or do not want to take. We all get so wrapped up in the need for more deductions. I find myself talking a lot about deductions, but the overarching question is do you need to spend the money?

I am never a fan of spending money you don't need to spend. I am a business owner. I am a cash flow strategist first and a tax consultant second. When clients come to me and say, "Should I lease or buy a car? Should I get a new truck?" my first question is always, "Do you need one? Do you need a new truck? Do you need a new computer?"

Yes, those items are deductible, but do you need to spend the money? I think that's a much more important question.

Our goal is always to take the money you are spending and turn it into a tax deduction and not spend more money to chase tax deductions. I would rather earn a dollar and give 40 cents to the government than earn nothing. You've heard and read many reports about,

"How do I pay no taxes?" Well, you make no money. That's never worked for me. Being homeless under a bridge to avoid taxes is not my plan.

I will help you plan to take all the money you are already spending to sustain our business and your life and make sure that you can deduct as much of that money as possible and not to chase additional deductions by spending money on things you don't need. That's where income tax planning and income tax strategies are so critical.

Strategizing, planning and recordkeeping all work together synergistically. Your tax accountant needs the entire, big picture to truly give you advice about minimizing tax due and maximizing deductions. We need to do the planning together.

When clients come in and I see that their office expenses are only $1000, for example, I'll say to them, "Where's the rest of it?" Very often, they've made a choice to run it on a personal credit card. Again, you must share all your information to identify deductions and reduce tax owed. If you do not want to use a separate credit card for business expenses, mark up your personal credit card statement to show your business expenses...keeping in mind ordinary and necessary. And, don't forget to retain receipts for all business items over $25.

Often, deductions are added money that you are spending anyway on the personal side that could be business deductions.

My advice in terms of planning and strategy is only to use personal money for truly personal expenses. Everything that belongs that your person, your hair, your clothes, your makeup, your gym, your groceries, your home, those are personal expenses and should be paid personally. Everything else that could be business-related should go to your business bookkeeping system. Your car, your gas in your car, your cellphone, your internet line, everything that you are spending which could be business-related should go to your bookkeeping systems so that you are arming your team to help you with strategies and planning.

If I don't see that data; if I don't see those numbers, it's very hard for me to do big-picture planning for you and maximize deductions in a vacuum. The hardest question I get is when someone shows me their profit and loss statement, and they say, "What else can I deduct?" That's just hard to answer because I don't know what else you're spending money on. I can only ask, what expenses are "ordinary and necessary" for you to run your business?

If you're running as many deductions as you can for your business, it is much easier for me to say to you, "Bob, these are not deductible. Come on. I see you putting those through your business. We can pull them out, reimburse them, and move them off the business financial statements." That is much easier for me to do than, in a vacuum, to say, "Well, gee, I don't know. Where is the rest of the money?" When you are erring on the side of running something through your business or not, I tell my clients to ask themselves two questions. Is this ordinary and necessary; could I make a case for this being deductible?

If In Doubt Add It

If you're at all in doubt, put an expense on the business so we can at least have that discussion. Again, my line in the sand is I do not want you to spend money you don't have to spend. I want you to have a successful business, pay as little tax as possible, and keep as much cash in your pocket as you can. That's the goal of strategic income planning for your taxes. Do not let a December 31st come and go without doing income tax planning. I can tell you that, almost every year on December 31st, I get a phone call from a client who says, "Oh no, I deposited a check. I wasn't thinking, and I was on the phone, and I put it in the ATM." Yeah, there's nothing I can do. Once it hits the banking system, you're paying tax on it. It happens every single year. Don't let that be you.

Last But Not Least Deduction Often Forgotten

I cannot complete the chapter on income tax planning without at least briefly mentioning the opportunities for business owners to contribute to pretax retirement accounts for themselves and their employees. These accounts can be extremely valuable deductions as they are allowed to be funded any time before your corporate or partnership income tax return is filed. This includes extensions.

So this deduction can minimize your income taxes and you only have to put the money into the retirement accounts in the following year before you file. I rarely recommend funding the accounts later for several reasons, the most prominent of which is that I recommend closing the year on December 31st and not dragging tax issues into the next year.

If you use next year cash for prior year retirement or taxes, then you find yourself in the often discussed "hamster wheel"; always chasing the net dollar. I prefer to be current and or ahead of all things cash and tax.

Now pretax retirement plans are complicated and the IRS imposed limits change every year. I recommend you meet with not only your account but also your financial advisor who will be the true expert in the different plans and how best to invest for your future retirement.

The three most common pretax retirement plans I recommend for my small business owners are:

1. SEP IRA
2. 401(k) Plan
3. Defined Benefit Plan

Pension Plan Characteristics -2018

SEP IRA		
Qualifications	**Contributions[1]**	**Deductions[1]**
Must be self-employed or work as an employee for an employer that contributes to a SEP on behalf of all eligible employees. An employer cannot discriminate against any employee at least age 21 who has worked three of the immediately preceding five years for the employer with at least $600 in compensation from the employer in 2018.	Must be identical percentage for all eligible employees. Must also contribute the same percentage for employees who separated from service prior to the end of the year [Proposed Reg. §1.408-7(d)(3)]. The employer does not have to contribute the same percentage each year as long as each employee receives the same percentage in any given year. Once contributions are made, the account is treated like a traditional IRA.	Contributions are deductible by the employer and are not included in the employee's W-2 wages

Qualified Plans

Qualifications	Contributions[1]	Deductions[1]
Self-employed individuals, partnerships, and corporations can set up qualified plans. Employees and partners of partnerships cannot set up qualified plans. If the plan is set up as a 401(k) plan, certain minimum coverage requirements apply. An employer can adopt a SIMPLE 401(k) plan that operates like a 401(k) plan without the minimum coverage requirement rules. A 403(b) annuity plan can only be set up by certain tax- exempt organizations and public schools. All qualified plans must allow employees at least age 21 with at least one year of service (minimum of 1,000 hours) to be eligible for participation in the plan. [IRC §410(a)]	Frequency and amount depends upon plan. Profit-sharing plans can change contribution percentages on a year-by-year basis. Money purchase plans must contribute the same percentage each year. Defined benefit plans depend upon a formula using a plan's current liability and the value of plan assets. Employee elective deferrals to 401(k) and 403(b) plans are at the discretion of the employee on a year-by-year basis. Employers are not required to match elective deferral contributions to 401(k) and 403(b) plans, except in the case of SIMPLE 401(k) and safe harbor 401(k) plans.	Employee elective deferrals are excluded from the employee's income. Employer contributions (including self-employed deferrals and matching contributions) are deductible by the employer. Employee elective deferral limits apply to all plans of the participant. For example, if a participant under age 50 in 2018 elects to defer $12,500 to the 401(k) plan of his first employer, the elective deferral limit for his second employer is $6,000 ($18,500 overall limit mi- nus $12,500). Likewise, if a self-employed individual under age 50 elects to defer $12,000 to his SIMPLE IRA, his elective deferral limit to a second job offering a 401(k) plan would be limited to $6,500 ($18,500 minus $12,000). [IRC §402(g)(3)]

Pension Plan Advantages/Disadvantages

Defined Benefit Plans	
Advantages	**Disadvantages**
Designed to provide a guaranteed monthly benefit for the life of a participant. The participant does not have to worry about outliving his or her retirement plan performance.	Fixed income could be inadequate in future years as inflation decreases the defined benefit.
Shareholder employees of closely held corporations can contribute and deduct more per year to a defined benefit plan than a defined contribution plan, in cases where the taxpayer wants to catch up on neglected retirement planning. Contributions for self-employed tax- payers are limited to 100% of compensation per year. [IRC §404(a)(8)	

A SEP IRA (a self-employed individual retirement account) is a written employer plan that allows you to make deductible contributions every year. This is the cheapest and most flexible option of the three. You can contribute some years and not others and you can contribute more dollars some years than others, depending on cash flow and income tax strategies.

Section 401(k) plans you may be familiar with from your days in corporate America as these are often found in large corporations but can absolutely be cost effectively introduced into your small business. I highly recommend this for business owners who have outgrown the SEP IRA above as they now have employees and are no longer "self-employed". Both you as the employer and your employee can make contributions to the plan each year. There are many more rules involved than with the SEP IRA and so this plan costs more money to maintain and requires additional tax filings with the government to stay in compliance.

The biggest and boldest plans are the third option, the defined benefit plan. My clients who want to contribute large sums of money, between $100,000 and $300,000, into the plan every year will select this plan as the costs of the plan which are substantial and run in the thousands are definitely worth every penny when the tax savings are in the tens of thousands if not more. Again, a large cash commitment is necessary and worth discussing depending on your needs for cash flow now versus retirement later.

I have a client who was faced with a large tax bill last year and so on December 26th, we called up and actuary and got a defined benefit plan set up and my client saved close to $100,000 in taxes. Sounds great right? Well no, not so much. This year, he has changed his focus and has decided to fund growth of a new service line within his business which is using up all available cash. He is not able to fund the defined benefit plan. Not good. Now his choice is to somehow between now and when we file the corporate tax return next year, come up with the cash for the plan, even the minimum payment which will likely be about $65,000 (and risk becoming the hamster in the wheel) or shut the plan down and risk the IRS coming back to him with a nasty letter and asking for their taxes back for the prior year. Tricky spot. So before jumping into this big hairy audacious defined benefit plan, please look forward and be sure you are ready for the commitment involved.

There are other options available too. Educated and experienced financial advisors are another highly recommended team member to work with all year long. Your financial advisor will be well positioned to discuss these and other pretax retirement options with you.

Remember, pretax now means taxable later. So you will also often here these plans referred to as deferral plans as you are deferring revenue from being taxable now to being taxable later. Upon retirement, these funds will become taxable.

And, I know it feels like I am being a downer on what just sounded like a brilliant tax plan but it is important for you to also understand that there are penalties involved in taking any of these monies form any of these three plans, or of your account before you retire. It gets expensive. So make sure that when you decide to enjoy this income tax deduction, that you are committed to locking up this money until retirement.

Last Word on Year-end Planning

And finally, I recommend that by December 25th, every year, you have a piece of paper in your hand or an email from your accountant that says, "Come April, this is what you're going to owe." We've already brought that date forward, and most of our clients now know that number by early December so they can plan for the holiday season. That way, you know how much you can spend over the holiday season. How much can you afford to spend versus what you are going to owe the government? It takes so much pressure off the holiday season if, by the first week of December, you know what you're going to owe in April. We figure that out together. What can you afford to spend on planning holiday gifts? These are critical numbers.

In the last quarter of the year, you absolutely must get a handle on what you're going to owe, how much cash you have, and what you can afford. Do not let December 31st come and go without doing any planning. If you take nothing else away from this entire book, and you learned nothing else, remember December 31st and remember me saying, strategic tax planning by December 31st is extremely important. Don't let it pass!

Our Unique Process

In my opinion, as a business owner, I work too hard to give money away in taxes. If you, too, want to make sure you have taken every business tax deduction to which you are entitled, and you want to keep more of your hard-earned money in your pocket, then I encourage you to implement all the tips and tricks covered in this book!

If you are ready to take the next step and work with a tax advisor who will show you how to maximize your deductions based on this book, then please reach out to us. We would love the opportunity to show you our strategies.

Schedule a deep-dive call with Wendy, for which there is no charge, to determine whether we are a good match for your needs. We will look at your cash flow and assess your risk tolerance.

After we have gone over your goals and current situation, we will offer strategies and tools that you may choose to implement based on your personal preferences. If you are a hard-working business owner and would like help in keeping more money in your pocket, we'd love to speak with you.

How Simple Tips and Tricks Can Help You Find More Tax Deductions for Your Business

Did you know that many small business owners in America are overpaying their taxes? The IRS publishes a list every year of deductions that taxpayers missed taking. And CPA's usually don't have the time to teach and explain so business owners turn to friends, colleagues or worse, google for tax advice.

Is this you? Are you overpaying your taxes? Want to learn how to take more deductions and keep more of your hard earned cash? This book will show you how!

If after you've read this book, you'd still like to learn more, go to my website **www.aboutprofit.com** to:

1. Download free worksheets

2. Sign up for our "That's Deductible!" online course

3. Schedule a One on One appointment with Wendy

My goal is to help you keep more of your hard earned cash by teaching you how to maximize your business income tax deductions. The next question is how will you spend all this extra money?